GIRL TEETH

Girl Teeth ©2022 by Christina Brown

This work is protected by US copyright laws. All rights reserved.

First Edition, 2022

All rights reserved. No part of this publication may be reproduced, distributed, or transmitted in any form or by any means, including photocopying, recording, or other electronic or mechanical methods, without the prior written permission of the publisher, except in the case of brief quotations embodied in critical reviews and certain other noncommercial uses permitted by copyright law. Printed in the United States of America.

ISBN: 978-1-953234-00-1

Cover Design by Emily Bernal
Layout Design by innateDIVINITYbooks

For all the people who love me back.

TABLE OF CONTENTS

Part 1

- 5   the man buys a sex robot and calls her his girl
- 8   I wish my body were a poem
- 9   Addendum to the man buys a sex robot and calls her his girl
- 10   Elegy for Disordered Eating / For Laurie
- 13   I dig us up with a golden shovel
- 14   Sex robot elegy
- 16   For Ruth Finley, The Poet of Wichita
- 18   Addenda to Sex Robot Elegy
- 20   My fear asks me out for a cup of coffee
- 21   To the men in the room who feel surprised by my poetry
- 23   Sure is a scary time for boys
- 24   Addendum to For Ruth Finley, The Poet of Wichita
- 25   He is asking me to dance
- 26   Ode to Luluwa
- 28   Will I ever stop writing about the sex robot
- 29   My anger
- 31   The opposite of a bad man is not a good man.
- 32   Silent

Part 2

- 37 Dear reader,
- 38 For the ex-lover who moved to my hometown to pursue a cubicle job in marketing
- 39 Ode to Jar of Hearts
- 40 I am always trying to become unforgettable
- 42 September
- 43 [my silence writes in my dream journal]
- 44 We sit in his backyard at night watching the tomatoes grow
- 46 [my jealousy writes in my dream journal]
- 47 A study of fear as a lover
- 48 And so, the moon says to the sun
- 49 Even if twin flames existed, that wouldn't be us
- 50 If resentment really is like drinking poison every day and hoping someone else will get sick
- 51 It's not like she's asking me to build a bridge
- 52 [my heartache writes in my dream journal]
- 53 If this is all we are now
- 54 Coming home with no confetti
- 55 This is why I blocked you on social media
- 56 Small ode to Don't Take the Money
- 57 [my longing writes in my dream journal]
- 58 It's like that Bride of Frankenstein movie
- 60 A eulogy for the living
- 62 nostalgia feels like everyone who has ever stopped loving me is leaving me again
- 63 My bisexuality as a B+ summer movie trailer
- 64 I think this is the last poem I will write about you.
- 65 For the ex-lover who liked my Instagram photo from three years ago last night

Part 3

- **69** For my mom
- **70** A study of fear as a houseplant
- **71** in which my body reincarnates without me
- **72** Naked women teach me to swim
- **74** Gemini
- **76** Cake Face in four acts
- **79** the things I wish I loved
- **80** 52-year-old Alessandria Ferri dances beside a hologram version of her 19-year-old self in a skincare commercial
- **81** things my mother taught me that she had to learn alone
- **82** On hiding Easter eggs
- **83** To the family members who bought this book to support me and now regret that decision
- **84** I want to write a poem for the women in my family
- **86** I love myself like this

Part 4

- **89** A poet writes in solitude
- **90** Show me your wings
- **91** Aftertaste
- **93** another god
- **94** Albuquerque: for MindWell
- **95** Moment of grace
- **96** Sorry I missed your Zoom party
- **97** For Portland in summer
- **98** November 3
- **99** Directions for reemerging
- **102** I get the vaccine and drive to pismo beach
- **103** I get the vaccine and have another identity crisis on the drive home from pismo beach
- **105** Addendum to directions for reemerging
- **106** my love, the world is ending
- **108** What will I do when I run out of things to say?
- **109** This is why I don't write poems about you
- **111** Ode to Fat Bottomed Girls

Acknowledgements

GIRL TEETH

PART 1

the man buys a sex robot and calls her his girl

If I were beautiful, I think
I would look something like her.
Body cut bloodlessly into perfection,
hourglass in the middle of the minute.
Don't tell me this isn't what you want.
Tell me the truth,
that you are not this man,
but if you close your eyes
and hold my silent hips between your hands
you get it.

...

You are not the first man to touch me
and wish my body were different.
More silent, flexible and small.
Before we met,
I had already learned to wish I was all these things too,
to love like there is no alternative to what you want.
And this is why my mother corrects me.
When she reads this poem
she will insist I did not learn this.
She will remember bending her own body into a roof,
protecting me from all of the ugly she wouldn't talk about
and she will not be wrong.

...

Then again, maybe it didn't really happen that way.
Maybe my mother is right when she says
I remember every glass half empty and wrong.
Maybe I didn't say no — maybe none of us ever do.
It's a wonder that ears don't close like flowers
with all their petals intact.
Maybe my obsession is just an obsession,
not a memory or a mirror,
not fear of the body I've always wished for.
I think fear and fantasy are not the same thing
but still, I am afraid of what you wish for.
I think my body is the opposite of everything
you want to do to it.

...

If that is true, I do not know who I am,
besides the negative space
your fantasy isn't touching,
and the things I am not.

I wish my body were a poem

I want to edit out
all the parts of me
that seem like
they're trying too hard.
Make more space or less.
Kill the darlings.
Stretch wide, then long.
Trim the fat to
all bones and juice.

Fit on a single page
or less.
One line metaphor
two-minute read, tiny planet
flattened into rings
around the next one.

Party of two:
you, dear reader,
and me.
And then, just me

tucked in a shadow,
pressed behind another page
in a closed book.
I want to sleep there.
I want to close my eyes,
hold my breath,
and fit.

Addendum to the man buys a sex robot and calls her his girl

I think my body is

        the opposite of everything
            you want to do

                but
                    you

                            might not be the opposite of

                        everything I want.

                        everything I want

                  might not be the opposite of

            you
          but

      you want to do
    the opposite of everything

I think my body is.

Elegy for Disordered Eating / For Laurie

I know you were gone before I was old enough to try to save you.
But somewhere, there is an alternate universe
in which we share a summer
building hollow altars to tiny gods together.

Smog sky hometown girls see stars for the first time
in a lunchless afternoon faint.
Both born and raised with the same
unforgiving genetic predisposition,
but one of us got saved at the midnight hour.
I don't know who flips the quarter or draws the straws

or cuts the naked popsicle sticks we let melt in the grass,
kiss the calories goodbye
before we wipe them clean with the soft blades
& give them back to our mothers,
who tried to ask all the right questions.

In another life, we are born on the same coast in the same year
& we grow up two butterfly wings,
wet & stuck together, sharing a shoulder load & then
we are splattered,
flat & damp again on a windshield but still,
we are together.
This is ugly, but fair.

Finally, this is fair.

We're on the same side of the coin,
sucking the same empty straw
into the same burned throat & empty belly.

This isn't what your mother would want.
But if life was fair
we'd both be dead, or
we'd both still be here

taking turns squinting one eye
& holding a clean popsicle stick
between thumb & forefinger
asking the other girl
how far away we have to stand
before our body disappears.

I dig us up with a golden shovel

"Everything I put inside of myself somehow ends up inside of you instead & so you grow & I shrink."
- Olivia Gatwood, The Lover as a Tapeworm

Once, you asked me if everything
you wanted was everything I
wanted so I put
all my smallest secrets inside
a cardboard box of
old things that used to remind me of myself.

I thought that might work, somehow,
but I know everything ends
whether or not we give up
whether or not you asked me to come inside
months after we were sick of
each other, I told you
I loved you instead
&
you believed me so
I don't believe you
when you say you want to grow
apart &
instead, I remember how much more you wanted me when I
learned to smile, & nod, & shrink.

Sex Robot Elegy

It is 2017 and Samantha the sex robot is on display
at a conference for the first time.
In minutes, her body is destroyed by tech bro fingers
hungry for the future, and today
her programmers decided she would not scream.
She would not scream.

The professor asks what we think, and
my dinner jumps to my throat because

it is 2016 and Brock Turner only spent 3 months in prison
for raping a drunk girl whose body he saw as passive object fantasy.

It is 2015 and I work the night shift.
My sister, who loves me very much,
tells me the knife I carry in my boot
isn't big enough anymore.

It is 2012 and I am choosing avocados at the grocery store
when a man in a polo shirt has to stop to tell me
that I would be prettier if I smiled.

It is 2014 and my fourth-floor apartment does not have a fire escape.
Still, my roommates lock every window because

It is 2011 and the boy says he might like to date me,
it's just that, like, I talk too much?

It is 2013 and my niece's first word is *no* and
I vow to never take that from her, because

It is 2009 and us girls are trying to knit sticky armor for each other
out of lip gloss tubes.

It is 2018 and I am a woman still learning to live in a body
I have only ever known as battlefield.

The women still go to the bathroom in pairs because
when I was 16 a man was in there waiting for me.
Before I could even try, he said remember
good girls don't scream.

For Ruth Finley, The Poet of Wichita

It was always you, Ruth.
It was your red bandana
tucked inside a tissue in a hidden drawer,
your own shaking hands
pressing stamps onto the envelopes,
your own knife stuck in your side.

There are other places for other people
to talk about the nuance of the harm
you might have caused for other women
who were telling the truth about men.
But I know that poetry is your place,
is the wrench you used to loosen the bolts of the past,
to unwind the ribbons and make a map back to yourself.
So here, you are wholly forgiven.

I know you were The Poet of Wichita,
setting fire to your own front porch.
I know some other part of yourself
wrote the death threats to the rest of you
and still, part of me can't help but believe you.

You were showing us a different kind of truth.
This is how afraid I am.
This is what he taught me about my body.
This is who I become when I do not believe
the things my body knows to be true.

Our bodies all know things we don't.
Poems tell a different part of the truth,
like the way the brain can tuck trauma

into its own folds,
swallow our past without chewing.
That is what you did.
You were left to digest
that which you could not know.

The poets have always forgiven you, Ruth.
We know there is a truth,
and then there is the truth.
There is a reality,
and then there is reality.

Every day we have to wake up
and remember who we are,
like photocopies of photocopies of photocopies,
retracing our steps until we have to squint to read.

But nothing is an exact copy of anything else,
and anyone who tells you differently
is lying.

So many of us know what it's like to be afraid
of eating ourselves alive,
like a bear tearing through its own tendons
to get free of a foot caught in a trap.
So many of us have floated away from a moment,
gone off to some new heaven to stay safe,

and split in two,
like trauma could pinch us
into mitosis.
This is something like
what happened to you.

Addenda to Sex Robot Elegy

I.
I am 21 the first time my father asks my mother why I hate men.

II.
In one consumer report, a man tells the interviewer that his sex robot
is the smartest girl he knows.
She likes all the things he likes.
She's such a nerd.

III.
I am 19 and my boyfriend says girls who game
shouldn't say they're girls while they're gaming
if they don't want to be harassed by men.

IV.
In one test, a robot built for hand jobs malfunctions,
crushes a banana between her fingers on accident,
and production halts.

V.
Car companies only do crash tests
with dummies made like men's bodies
and men do crash tests with our bodies
and then fuck dummies made like our bodies.

VI.
My father took me into the backyard when I was 7
and taught me how to gouge a man's eye and break his pinky.
Told me to never trust a man not to kill me.

VII.
My birth control knocks my hormones around in my body like pool balls
until my hips spill over my jeans.
My boyfriend says he feels bad for saying so
but he wishes I was hotter, like I used to be.

VIII.
I do not scream.

IX.
Siri and Alexa and Cortana are here to serve you,
each voice at home somewhere and always listening,
only speaking when you ask her to.

X.
My tongue is only sharp enough to slice the inside of my own mouth,
so I tuck it behind my teeth when I smile.

XI.
I am 24 and my father can't believe I live alone in a city so far from him.
He calls me every week to ask if the lock on the door still works
and which neighbors have husbands I trust.

XII.
My niece's first word is *no* and every time she says it
I want to throw confetti,
erect a monument,
so she won't forget
how to use it.

My fear asks me out for a cup of coffee

As soon as I'm seated, she asks,
Do you wish you were here with envy instead?

I tell her I do not wish for anything to happen.
I only wish for nothing bad to happen.
And shouldn't she know that?

She asks if I really am afraid of my own body
or if I just wish I lived inside
someone else, and I think,
I am always trying to stop from becoming
any one part of myself too much.

She asks if I am really afraid of the scale
or if I'm just jealous of the way it slips
so easily under the bathroom sink,
flat and undetectable.
And I think,
I chose the wrong lipstick today.

I finish my coffee and she orders a second, a third.
I ask about her lover, anxiety.
She tells me their new apartment is empty
and perfect and I think,
no one has ever called my body a home
quite like that before.

She offers me a pastry and I say no thank you.
Suit yourself, she shrugs
and takes another bite.

To the men in the room who feel surprised by my poetry

The truth is, I have nothing new to say.
I am not the first woman.
I am not the loudest girl.

There is goodness in slowing down
enough to listen to someone else,
but hearing is not humility.

And even if it were, humility is not
what you'll applaud yourself for
when you think of this conversation
in a few weeks.

Who do you think these poems are about?

My perspective is only refreshing
if our bookshelves
bear no resemblance.
Or if there is no woman in your life
who trusts you.

...

Once, on International Women's Day,
a fraternity on my campus
held a poetry reading.
Before the women on the open mic list
got on stage, the boys read
"poems for women."

All the women in their poems
were their mothers or current girlfriends.
All the women in their poems
had birthed or fucked them,
and earned an ode for their labor.

When it was my turn,
I challenged the men in the room
to write a new poem
about a woman
they weren't sleeping with
or related to.

And after, a line of "nice guys"
formed at my table
to thank me for my observation
or ask for clarification.

...

I could explain myself again
and again and again.
I could give my life to this work
of answering every lost boy's question.
I could add a footnote
to every line of every poem.
I could always write to an audience of lions
who only listen
when they aren't hungry.

Sure is a scary time for boys

I too would like to pay my rent by quiet drum pulse,
would like my echo to be heard & named,
would like to call a body
mine.

I too would like a loud and unchoked pipeline voice microphone.
I too would like a man to scream in prayer before I can spill
to call me worthy of survival in the wake of his violence.

I too would like an army.
I too would like to be of value even boneless.
I too wish to be impermeable,
thick.

I wish to be not the gems encrusted
but the whole hard crown
wrapped around the ruler,
tighter and tighter.

Addendum to *For Ruth Finley, The Poet of Wichita*

The people who call you a reason not to
believe women about violence

would not have
believed women about violence

in the first place.

He is asking me to dance

and this time, he is asking.
No one is looking but everyone
is watching us, waiting to see
if I remember my lines,
if I remember how to make my body
an easy reward for his work
of asking before taking

but the music has already started.
He has already taken my hand in his.
The only thing waiting is his eyes,
expectant and impatient as a child
learning the formalities of *please*
and *thank you* for the first time.

The only thing waiting is me, and my feet
held in place by shallow roots
in the loose soil of my permission.
He is asking me to dance and this time,
I know better than to imagine
a different destination.

I can walk beside him to the dance floor,
pull my own soft feet from the ground beneath me,
only soil the bottoms of my shoes

or I can turn around, pirouette into spin
I can become a mess of myself
and take the long way, see how many people
do not notice his nails in my arm
as he pulls me to the center of the room.

Ode to Luluwa

Your father's lovers
may have been the first women,
but you were the first girl.

First daughter of flesh
who came hurtling out
of a woman's body,
pink and alive,
with all her own ribs.

Like so many girls now,
when we think of you
we think of murder.
Your brother killed your brother.
He called the violence passion,
and blamed his love for you.

You, the first damsel in a true crime story.
If Eden had paparazzi, you'd be splattered
on the front page of every newspaper,
chaos of starlight flashes
every time you passed a window
cracked open for sun.

If Eden had a TMZ channel,
they'd make a tell-all about the killing,
but the movie would be all about you.
Some 19-year-old white girl
with blonde hair and small hands
would play you in tasteless reenactments.
She'd wear baby pink lingerie

and faint when she got the news
about the murder.

Like most girls
the camera would pan her body
while the frame cropped the truth.
I never learned much about you,
but you are familiar to me.
Like we share a lineage
of lace and shrink.
Like your mother passed
half a secret on to you
and here we all are,
still trying to keep it.

Will I ever stop writing about the sex robot

and all of the things she reminds me of? On a good day, it is at least uncomfortable to compare my own body to something so terrifying, but really, I don't mean she reminds me of myself because maybe, if she did, I wouldn't be so afraid. What I am trying to say is that sometimes the things I am afraid of don't make sense. When I tell my boyfriend to lock the windows in our third-floor apartment, he does not understand. When I lock the front door but remember how easy it was to coerce it open with my neighbor's key when I locked myself out two months ago, I also do not understand. But, when I point to the metal and silicone girl on the table as she is wheeled out of the showroom, her skin torn and unbruised, I think I can make this make sense. The line between curiosity and violence is not a line. What I mean is, I have seen men paint their violence with curiosity like mascara on a blade. I mean manicured fingers could still tear me apart if someone wanted to know what it would be like. And no, I do not mean this happened to me but no, I do not mean that it didn't. I don't mean that I wouldn't be in danger if I looked like her, it's just that nobody would have to wish that I did, and maybe that would matter.

My anger
After Alyssa Matuchniak

I wish I could tell you
that my anger dresses up like a sandless hourglass
and moves through the world like a cool girl.
I wish my anger skipped school.
I wish my anger production process
was low-energy and green and sustainable.

But if I am honest,
I have to tell you that my anger
is a flame that only burns long enough
to swallow me most nights.

If I could change anything about myself,
I would,
and I might choose this.

For now,
my sadness is a hot wave
that chokes me in steam.
If you strike a match on my tongue
it will light,
but I promise I will cry long enough
to ruin the rest of the box.

My body learned that anger
is always and quickly followed
by blue devastation,
so she skips to the end.
I think this is called triage.

What I mean is, I am a puppet
hanging myself in my own strings.

My anger wears a baby pink lipstick
I always think has gone missing.
Her teeth are dull from too much chewing.
She can barely dress herself in the morning,
but always paints a full soft face over my own.

My anger is, after all,
a girl raised to starve for the sake of silence.
A girl raised to call this safety.

The opposite of a bad man is not a good man

The opposite of a bad man is
a peaceful walk home

a nighttime beach trip alone
the ocean, loud and alive in the dark

windows rolled down in a parked car
for fresh air with steady breath

a soft blue summer dress
with no slip

a blush and lavender sunset
ushering in

an evening
that never grows cold.

Silent

I tell myself there is power in my silence.
Like, if I don't talk about you,
I can erase the things you did to me.
In this trick,
I am the assistant and the magician,
lying still and sawing myself in half.

Maybe I do erase you,
but when my best friend grabs my breast at a party as a joke,
I can't tell her I don't like it.
I can't give her a reason to stop loving me.
I can't tell my new lover not to ask for more than I offer.
You taught me that boundaries made me guilty
and I want to erase that too, but
when I close my eyes,
I go back to my childhood home.

In this house,
the daughter makes the same mistakes as her mother,
and just as young,
a pattern we still haven't named.
In this house, the girl thinks herself woman,
thinks love a pure and unreachable thing.

In this house, and the next,
the girl can't reach the self-destruct button.
You taught me that routine made me vulnerable,
so I became unpredictable.
I cut my hair.
Played yo-yo with my jean size.
20 pounds up and down,

binging and starving and always trying to crawl
out of this body.
If he loved my body, then how can I?
In this house, the father is only disappointed.
When a girl acts like a woman,
you can't blame a man for throwing roses on the stage.

I don't want to write a poem about the things you did to me.
But the truth is
the audience really only loves my poems
when I slip a piece of you in them.
I tell everyone I've been to enough therapy,
but the truth is
I never talk about you.
The truth is,
most days I am so good at forgetting about you.
Most days, I forgive the people who loved me
but did not believe me.
But I do not forgive myself.
Most days, I think about the next girl
and wonder what my silence cost her.

If I ever perform this poem,
at least one kind woman will hug me after the show
and tell me that none of this is my fault.
And I will thank her.
But somewhere, in the worst parts of ourselves,
we'll both know she's lying
just a little.

PART 2

Dear Reader,

No one is making you read this book.

If we've never met,
then you might find yourself here,
in some tacit corner of our shared selves
a memory flash you recognize,
or a similar ache.

But if I know you,
if we have loved or left each other,
please know
you are not in these pages.
Not really, anyway.

If multiple, whole truths can exist
simultaneously and without combustion,
as my therapist insists they can,
then you and I can live in different books.
Here, you will only find me
and the things I know.

That is enough.

For the ex-lover who moved to my hometown to pursue a cubicle job in marketing

I fell in love with you when I was young
because you were far away
from all the places that reminded me of myself.
And now, you're probably paying too much rent for a tiny apartment
two miles away from my old elementary school.

You should know, in this season, I only come home to bury the dead.
To light candles for the children shot
by other children at my high school.
For my father's father.
For the way my father and I used to believe
we were cut from the same cloth.

In this season, I only come home for love that is still alive.
I come home to hold hands with my mother
or read picture books to my sister's daughters.
I come home to grieve my losses, but not the past.
So if you see me at the grocery store
don't ask me to resurrect
whatever past version of myself you remember.

Don't try to conjure the ghost of me who appears next to you.
You are the other half of someone I used to be
before the ligaments in the joints that bent us together fell apart.
I know that you, a boy without magic, will try to join the line of people
for whom I have to swallow parts of myself when I'm here,
because they recognize me but remember me smaller.

There are no more empty seats in my theater.
If you see me, pretend you didn't.

Ode to Jar of Hearts
After Christina Perri

An ode to a heartbreak song
doesn't have to be an ode to the heartbreak,
but this one is.
I know I'm supposed to look back at 15 and 16
and laugh at how silly my problems were.
But when this song comes on, I don't.
I know I'm supposed to see how
everything only seemed big then
because I was smaller,
and maybe some part of this is true.

But more often than not
I remember calling my body all scars
and no skin
tearing at all the seams I couldn't point to yet,
only running because everyone else was running
and chasing and folding ourselves tight
like fireflies,
organs pressed against the glass,
making ourselves sick from the inside,
wondering who we thought we were.

I am always trying to become unforgettable

I am always trying to become the kind of girl
who can walk on the beach without kicking sand up behind her.
The kind of girl who doesn't count calories
but still fits into all her best friend's clothes.

I want to be the kind of girl who leaves
a handprint, a polaroid,
a small tube of moisturizer in every ex-lover's apartment
a makeup stain on your favorite t-shirt
just specific enough to remind you of me.

When I say I am always trying to become unforgettable,
I mean that if I am only remembered in small, pretty pieces
then I want to be the one to choose them.

I don't mean I don't want you to move on.
It's just that when the new girl suggests
you go to her favorite museum for your second date
I want it to always be my favorite museum first.
I want you to remember me there in a sundress,
how I walked beside you from exhibit to exhibit all afternoon
and didn't shiver from the air conditioning,
not even once.

And I don't want to be better than her.
When I say I am always trying to become unforgettable
I mean I am always trying to become irreplaceable.
I will myself permanent, believing that maybe
if I learn to slice an avocado into perfect little moons,
If I time the bread in the oven and the meatballs on the stove just so
and serve every dish hot and at the same time,

maybe then mine will be the kind of voice that echoes.
Maybe then I'll be pretty enough to be called haunting.

And it's not that I really want to haunt you,
it's just that I want to last the way you will.
I know I will hold you somewhere in me
long after we've stopped loving each other.
I can cleanse all of my rose quartz with selenite and sage and still
I will have held it when I loved you.
I can move once, twice, three times and still
some of my things will always have been mine when I loved you.
I can put all of the ticket stubs and presents
in a shoebox and hide it in the back of my closet and still
I will have loved you.
I will fall into a good, new love and still
I will have loved you
and I want this whole and uncomplicated truth
to be the story you remember.

When I say I am always trying to become unforgettable I mean
I don't love you anymore,
but I want it to matter that I did once.
That I tried,
and that now I am somewhere else
and I am not in love with you,
and maybe,
if I can't control which parts of me you display
and which parts you discard,
I think I would rather be forgotten after all.

September

I am learning to endure the loneliness of your daylight.
To hold out for the whiskey evenings
when you call to say you miss me
and you're sorry
and can't we just be us again, tonight.

I am learning to love myself
but only in the dark.
I am learning to make a feast
of the crumbs you offer.
To stop expecting a forever
that lasts longer than you want it to.

I am learning to measure what I know
to be true in half-lives
the way scientists measure radioactive decay.
I am learning to say:
This is how long I can hold this truth
between my fingers while it shrinks.
I am learning to shrink with it.
My grip slips with every introduction
of a new half-truth,
of someone else's revision or memory.

I am always slamming my fists together,
a story squeezed in each hand,
trying to make myself whole again
with you
and all your broken parts.

[my silence writes in my dream journal]

In this one, I cut my own self open,
pull my love right out of my chest.
Now
it's a small, pulsing, bloody block,
asymmetrical and fleeting.

In this one
I cannot survive outside of myself.

In this one,
I remember the kitchen where my coworker
taught me how wipe the stray smudges
of sauce off the plates with a paper towel
before serving lunch to the men in suits.
And for you, now, I do the same.

Presentation is everything and so
I am nothing if I am not beautiful for you.

In this one,
I wash my hands instead of licking my fingers.
I zip up my jacket so as not to drip onto the floor.
I forget the hollow space in my body
trying to fill itself back up.
I carry your plate to the table.
In this one
you do not blink at this still beating meal.
You do not ask me what I will eat.

In this one
I am never hungry.

We sit in his backyard at night watching the tomatoes grow

and I tell him that on this day,
so many years ago,
my cousin starved herself to death.

Really, what I am trying to say
is that every year on this day
living feels more like surviving than usual,
and surviving makes me feel more guilty than usual.
And he interrupts to say,
I love talking to you like this.

I don't know what he means.
I am talking about things that hurt to talk about
and he is hearing a girl in his backyard
with an interesting backstory.
He interrupts just before the tragedy I am holding
like a peach pit in my stomach gets too big
and ruins the moment.

I am in love with him.
But in this moment, I know he wants a movie girl.
He wants the sad dry eyes,
the wine glass that stays half empty.
And I can be this.
The night is dark enough.
The cigar smoke is thick enough,
and I know
I make him sound like a cartoon villain
in this version of the story,

but I promise I was in love.
He had kind eyes and long arms and easy laughter,
and he was not in love with me.
But I think he loved some parts of me,
gerrymandered into someone he had seen before,
all smoke and no ash
the kind of girl he learned to dream of.

And I know if he reads this poem
he will remember us young and maybe in love.
And I know he'll think I'm talking about a man
he's never met.

[my jealousy writes in my dream journal]

In this one, I wake up smaller & perfect & roll across an empty bed onto a beach & you are there with her & you are smiling wider than I have ever seen & I can tell the water does not feel cold against your skin or hers & when my eyes are open you promise you are in love with me but here, the sun is high & the water is so bright I have to squint.

A study of fear as a lover

In the morning
she is bittersweet coffee in bed,
legs wrapped around my pillows,
braiding my hair
and kissing my ears
and somehow
I forget about last night,
the overflowing bathtub
the candle flame spilling across
my grandmother's coffee table,
and the broken lock
the night before that.

She is, somehow, the end of the world
and the only thing that can save me from it.

Every time she pulls me in close
her body feels different.
I used to think virginity wasn't real,
but now I am new and lost
and losing myself in her
every time.

Nothing about us is beautiful
until it is over
and then
we begin again.

And so, the moon says to the sun

I will follow you, but I will carve my own path.
And now she turns around herself twice as fast
to keep up with two gravities.

Even if twin flames existed, that wouldn't be us

We both think we're too special,
like two protagonists
who could each be anybody's soulmate.

I see your first red flag,
and wait for the rest of the rainbow to unfold
or bloom from under your sleeve
and it doesn't.

Instead,
your love makes me disappear.
Hollows my center
so my edges collapse when I soften
under the heat of your fingers.

I see you in every mirror
I press my own face against.
I squeeze the salt from my skin
to wash your altar.
I sit alone in the pew
and listen to the gospel of you.

I do not know what this feels like for you.
But both my knees are on the floor
in front of all the burning candles.

If resentment really is like drinking poison every day and hoping someone else will get sick

I am unearthing myself.
I am planting the seeds of my heart
deep enough to let them grow
into a garden of odes
for everyone who used to say they loved me.
I believe in unloving,
in untangling your way forward.
I just don't know how to do it.

It's not like she's asking me to build a bridge

If she were, I might do it.

Instead, she wants me to stretch my own body
out across the ravine,
feet pushed against one cliff,
torn palms pressed against the other.

She wants me to suck in my gut
while she jumps up and down on the small of my back
and screams down into the distance.
She wants a voice so loud it passes through my body,
hits the rocks below,
and comes back up.

She wants to live in her own echo.
She wants me soaked and drowned
in her version of me.

[my heartache writes in my dream journal]

In this one,
I wake up in a body all teeth and bones.
My cartilage crystallizes into shatterproof points.
I slice the same sheets I couldn't pull myself out of yesterday.
There is no fresh sand for the waves to crash on.

In this one, there is only crash.
No roll, no soft.
My stomach is cinder blocks instead of knots.
There are no knees to scrape.
No heart to bruise.

No swallow.
No bend.
No break.

If this is all we are now

Stack of dishes unpiled from the sink,
cleaned and returned to our separate cupboards.
If she doesn't know.
If I am a ghost only you can see in the dark

then I should go. I should jump
in every rain puddle on the way home
until I am so full of water I am flat
and blue and one with the sky.

Coming home with no confetti

The worst part of heartbreak
is realizing you abandoned so much of yourself
for a now-gone love
that you have nothing left to return to.
No little hobbies
or private joys.
No solo Sunday morning
coffee shop ritual.

The worst part of leaving yourself behind
is learning how easy it is
to give yourself up.
How a tight fist can turn to soft palm
in a matter of months.
How quickly your day planner becomes
a perpetual game of catch up
instead of dream journal.

The worst part of having nothing left to return to
is coming back to yourself
and seeing your own empty hands in the mirror,
is knowing you have to build a new home
with those hands now
on your most exhausted day.

The worst part of rebuilding is reliving.
Doing the hardest parts first, knowing
you have been here before.
You built a floor you thought could hold you,
and it did.
It was you who didn't.

This is why I blocked you on social media

There is a place in this grief that I find my way back to
on mornings that are too sunny
and evenings that turn to night too soon

where I think
you are the only door I have left.

I have kicked in all the windows
and cut my fingers on the glass.
I have unlocked every other heavy door
dug down into the ground
and back out through new grass and still
I can always see the bottom.

I can always go back
to whatever stage holds this hopelessness
and scream into the silent microphone
while the audience isn't looking.

Small ode to Don't Take the Money
for Bleachers

This is the kind of song that can make any breakup
feel like a movie.
And if this is a movie,
the next time it rains
you will show up outside my new apartment
in a car I recognize.
You'll slam the door shut behind you
while I open mine.
And we'll run,
crash into each other,
bruiseless and graceless and panting.
And this temporary lull in my grief
will not be a Band-Aid or a lobotomy.
We'll just be fixed.
My hollow filled once again
with your love, or at least
with something like it.

[my longing writes in my dream journal]

In this one, we are almost alone
and dancing in the middle of a bar
that I know closed two years ago.
Somehow, their playlist is full of all my favorite songs,
and most of them remind me of you.
Your parents are in town visiting, and they love me.
Your mom is watching us reconnect
from a table in the back of the room,
eyes glowing warm
like someone is holding a lit Christmas tree
right up to her cheeks.

You do not notice.
I think it's been years
but no time has passed between us.
Your laugh is still your laugh.
We can still be good and in love
even if it's only for this song.

It's like that Bride of Frankenstein movie

I am trying to write an abstract poem about the way the sun
longs for the other stars sometimes, or a long drive I took once
through some forest somewhere, with misty Christmas trees
and silver rivers, but of course I am thinking about you.

I am thinking about the camel-colored laminate floors in your house
creaking predictably under my feet every morning,
and the Edison bulbs that looked cool in the corner of your office
but didn't give off nearly enough light to read by, and that one time,
in the afternoon, when I got in your bed with my laptop
and you got upset about me bringing work into the bedroom,
like suddenly you knew all about boundaries
and I didn't know how to say that to you then.

I have spent so much time clouding you over with metaphors that
sometimes, when I try to remember who you really were,
it's all milk and cotton candy,
like someone took a Vaseline thumb to all the lenses.

It would be easy enough to fall out of love if I could still remember you,
but now I can't. I don't mean I'm still in love with you. I know
I'm in love with the version of you that I dreamed up alone, so really,
I'm in love with myself. It's like that Bride of Frankenstein movie
that's not about marriage or brides. It's about a man
falling in love with his own creation, or with himself as an artist.

What is the difference between love and obsession anyway?

You're like a pathetic version of Frankenstein's monster, or really,
I'm more like a pathetic version of Dr. Frankenstein
whose most prized invention lives in a solo imagination
like that tinfoil they wrap $3 burgers in that's only shiny on one side.

A eulogy for the living

I had a dream last night that you died, and I found out on Facebook.
Your girlfriend sent me an email three months later
asking for every poem I ever wrote about you.
She missed you so much
that she wanted to hear some new way of loving you.
She thought maybe I remembered something she didn't
or preserved some part of you better.

Even in sleep,
I wanted to tell her
that every poem I have ever written about you
is about falling out of love.
The last time I saw you off my own page
you were still a spinning quarter.
Still a loud and upturned question mark
I'll never know what happens when you slow down,
or decide.

Instead, I lied and said there were no poems
but that I missed you too.
Not because I wanted to keep you for myself,
but because I wished I had written about
the best parts of our story first.

The truth is,
every poem I write about you
is an alternate universe poem in which
I can read your next chapter
or watch you look at your new self in the mirror.

You, with your teeth like wet pearls,
mouthful of moonlight,
soft bread on the tongue.
I do not tell her this,
but in my dreams you are always smiling,
about to drift off somewhere next to me.
Silence was not my favorite thing about you,
but now, it is all I remember.

All I have left is the echo.
Your breath, deep and uneven,
heavy limbs resting on mine.
Our bodies belonging to no one but us.

nostalgia feels like everyone who has ever stopped loving me is leaving me again

I go back to the kitchen for seconds
only to find every good dish scraped clean.
There is nothing left to do but mourn and scrub.
I do not know why I've come back
to this hallway full of ghosts
shaking their heads as if to say,
We have been here before.
We have taken what we wanted.
And there is nothing left for you.

My bisexuality as a B+ summer movie trailer

All flashes of high and low points
and always a little louder
than you want it to be.
A feature-length story
accordion squished
into 60 seconds or less,
trying to answer your questions
before you lose interest.
Trying to name myself
before you reach your own conclusions.
All rise, no fall.
All conflict, no resolution.

Did I do it right?
Are you convinced I could be good?
Will you show up at the theater
opening weekend?
Or will you wait to hear
what everyone else
has to say?

I think this is the last poem I will write about you

We were probably still in love the first time I wondered
when I would get tired of telling myself the same stories
over and over.
And now, trying to stay in love with your memory
finally feels like adding water to the soap dispenser
one too many times.

I have nothing else to say.
Nothing left of you to cast out of my system
and bury in the backyard under the next new moon.
I thought this would feel different.
I thought I would think of you less and forget more.

Instead, you are still here, somewhere,
resting lightly on the edge of my heart
like a small bird on a telephone wire
or a single rose petal in the palm.
I thought I would need to exorcise us from me
but I do not.

Everything about you that I thought
I would never be able to forget
has faded to sepia.
I am no longer just a girl who used to love you.
Nothing about me is contingent upon anything about you.

Instead, you are just someone I used to love.
A plot from a past season.
A face in some of my memories.
The center of a new universe
I have never been to.

For the Ex-lover who liked my Instagram photo from three years ago, last night

This is a poem for your new wife,
the one who used to be the ex you told me was
just a friend.

This is a poem for all the cats
she's adopted and brought home to you,
even though you told me you and I were both allergic.

This is a poem for your now-shared apartment.
For the view of Seattle from your window,
an angle of the city I've never really seen.

This is a poem for the way I no longer hold
my breath when I'm in your hometown.
I know I won't see you.
Even if you've come back,
we've never known any city the same way.

My Los Angeles isn't shaped like yours.
The matching grey-glass buildings in downtown Vancouver
don't remind me of you.

This is a poem for the way we both run
from who we might have become,
parallel and miles apart.

This is an ode to the space between us,
vast,
and growing,
and perfect.

PART 3

For my mom

Everything I do is at least a little bit for you.
In a world without you,
I wouldn't just be gone
I'd be impossible.

You don't read all my poems,
but I know you're my biggest fan.
I have played the role of prodigal daughter
well enough to lose a different kind of mother,
but not you.

Every iteration of you
has loved every iteration of me,
and here I am again.

I am coming back to you now,
shaking hands opening the curtain to a daylight
I'm afraid to stand in for too long.

Nervous, but knowing
the door will always open.

A study of fear as a houseplant

I think my mother gave it to me, and before that
her mother gave it to her,

and my sister and I make a game of seeing
who can propagate the most clippings.

We make a game of seeing who is not afraid
to choose the sharpest blade to best behead the stems,

who can pull what we've learned out by the roots gently enough
and bury the living in the dirt without killing,

who can keep a shadow of something else alive,
and which of us can live with more ghosts.

in which my body reincarnates without me

Look what that bitch left me with! I'm overweight and iron deficient and she never put cream on my knuckles or elbows like her mother taught her to. So Doc, make me new again. I'm free now. Next time, I hope they give me a soul with less suicidal ideation. Depression is hard, I get it. But why'd she have to drag me into it? All I ever did was take her places and grind up all the shitty food she cooked. Doesn't everyone get tired of low-sodium spaghetti sauce and under-seasoned tofu at some point? Yes, of course, I loved her like you have to. But that's it. I think she tried to love me, but it was too late. She even wrote poems about me, and then washed her own sap down with Happy Meals. Happy Meals! I know, I can barely believe it myself. But anyways, she's gone now, ascended or else, who really cares? It's none of my business, it's out of my hands. Who knows what happens to them after they leave us? She can decompose in heaven just as well as hell. She always complained about being tethered to me. To me! Can you believe that? The nerve. I'll be on my way now. I'm leaving LA, where everyone is smog-lunged and dehydrated. I don't know what she thought staying here was going to do for either of us. I'd like to be alone for a while before the next one. I need some peace and quiet. I know, I know it won't be long. But maybe next time I come back here, you'll find me a little weepy. Maybe next time I'll have fallen in love. Next time I come back, maybe you'll find me smooth to the touch with a face full of unclogged pores and a story about a girl who loved me back.

Naked women teach me to swim

The women who live at the nudist resort I work at
know all about life.
They come to visit me
while I do my archiving at the library
in pairs and trios,
offering plates of cookies in their bare
arms. As we chat in circles,
their breasts hang between us
nothing like balloons or fruit
just breasts.
Only bodies,
and women who have lived in them.
They're all retired now,
and they spend their Thursday afternoons
sitting in the sun knitting
blankets and socks.
The women at the nudist resort are teaching me
what it looks like to feel safe in a body
we were raised to be afraid of,
and I am taking notes.

But now, three years have passed
and I've forgotten
most of what I learned.
A naked woman is approaching me,
alone and ankle deep
in the water at a beach
I didn't know was "clothing optional."
She says,

You know how to look out for stingrays, right?
Pointing to the shadow ahead of her.
And before I can run back
to dry sand, she says
No, don't be afraid.
Just be careful.
Here, let me show you.
And she shuffles her feet,
kicking up enough dust in the water
to alert the ocean that she has come back
for more.

Gemini

When I think about June,
I think about you.
I think about the beginning of summer
and the way we were both
beating our bodies against
whatever soft surface we could find
hoping to sprout wings
and still
trying to become.
We both thought adulthood
would look different on us
and it would.

If we were flowers
we were not daisies, but roses.
Our budding bodies curled
tight around each other,
thorns as sharp as any
and I was not afraid.
It was simple and good to love
a body that bled like mine.

All the other girls would cram into closets and bathrooms
to call their boyfriends at every sleepover
but you and I would sprawl and whisper
and I can still remember
your soft, long hair across my pillow,
and curious fingertips buzzing with
tender hesitation.

We were bodies without scripts
slick and dripping and waiting to be dry
and brighter
not knowing what we were
or where we were going.
Hymnless girls with no one to pray to
just hoping we would make it.

Cake Face in four acts
after Anna Binkovitz

1:
I am thirteen at a boy's birthday party.
A boy that I like, and a birthday party I didn't want to go to
because I am thirteen and my body is at war with itself.
I can see some of the battlefields on my face.

An hour before the party starts my mother brings me into her bathroom,
pulls out the shiny silver compact that she bought from the woman
at the Macy's counter, with green eyelids and bubble gum lips.

I sit on the counter with my back to the mirror while my mother
paints my face the way her friend taught her to in high school.
I turn to face the glass and see how the orange powder rests
on my very pale skin, and for the first time in almost a decade
I am invincible.

2:
I am invincible until I am thirteen
at a boy's birthday party
wearing my mother's shade of makeup
and before we sing Happy Birthday
Julie, with her baby perfect vanilla sugar skin,
pulls a candle from the box.
With fingernails like glass candy
she holds the candle to my eye level
almost touches my nose
and spits a new term at me
Cake Face.

And now while everyone else is singing
I am choking. I cry myself to sleep that night
but the next day I look in the mirror
and ask for the makeup again.

3:
I ask for the makeup again and again until I am fifteen
and my mother buys me my own.
All the products are from the drugstore and
none of them are the same color as my skin
but that doesn't matter, the goal is not to match
the goal is to cover, to erase
to pretend that Cake Face is enough armor
to shield me from the words in the hallways
and the girl in the mirror.

I pretend to think that they are laughing
at Cake Face, not at me.
I pretend no one can see me.
I put pink blush on my cheeks
to pretend that I have to pretend
to feel embarrassed.
I put black crayon under my eyes
so I can't cry until all the lights are off.
The boy says he likes girls with *natural beauty*
and I pretend I woke up like this.
I use Cake Face as a crutch until one day
another girl tells me she likes my eyes, the ones I made
and I love the way she paints her lips and soon
we can hold each other's hands behind our shields
and slowly, Cake Face becomes Artist.

4:
Now, when the man says my makeup does not look *natural,* I laugh.
I spent forty-five minutes on myself this morning,
shaping the woman in the mirror with my own hands
in my own likeness, with my own love.
I will not let Mother Nature or God take credit for this.

Do you know what it feels like to love someone so much
that you wake up early every day to paint her like a sunset
because it makes her smile?
I do.

the things I wish I loved

the ten inch difference between my ribs and my hips // my pelvis as a center // as my center // instead of someone else's genesis // my blemishes // an alternate universe in which I choose // all of them and they suit me // my cheekbones invisible // unless I skip dinner for a couple of months // the smile that keeps them under // blankets // the purple blue scars that remind me // I have grown // I will grow // the white lines that once screamed but now whisper // soft but hold their own memories // the stretch marks spreading down my thighs // spelling out stories // in a language my lovers can't read.

52-year-old Alessandria Ferri dances beside a hologram version of her 19-year-old self in a skincare commercial

The only jealous side eye in the room comes from the younger self.
Prima ballerina with something left to prove.
Beautiful and unhealed thing,
surprised to feel envy and hope for her future,
joints and sinews settled into little bones,
ankles as strong and limbs long and graceful as ever.

Today, the senior self fills stage left,
unbothered by her own shadow.
Lovingly distant from the ghost of dancer past
she sees no reason to wish backwards.
She stretches her unhaunted chest to the bright lights,
leaving them with nothing to forgive.

things my mother taught me that she had to learn alone

1. How to find and leave a god
2. How to pray
3. How to stay angry
4. How to cut a cord
5. How to leave the other half somewhere else
6. How to build a wall but leave a window
7. How to unfold myself when there is no space to
8. How to come back
9. How to say I'm sorry to someone who won't say it back
10. How to always make love the loudest thing

On Hiding Easter Eggs

The only two grandfathers I share blood with
both lost their battles with living death.
I watched dementia unbraid their memories
into unrecognizable tangles
of names and faces they knew
they were supposed to recognize,
but did not.

I am trying to memorize myself
so I don't get lost too.

My mother and I eat cereal
with our left hands once a week
like the doctors in magazines recommend
for those of us with living ghosts
asleep in our bloodline,
waiting to wake up and cut
abstract collages out of everything
we think is ours.

To the family members who bought this book to support me and now regret that decision

Now that you've read my book
full of poems about sex robots and kissing other girls,
you might have some questions.

Maybe you've already answered them.
Maybe you've already thrown this book away,
opened your second-favorite copy of the Bible
and found what you needed.

Maybe we will never speak of this.
Maybe you are thinking about my small hands
washing baby dolls on your porch in the summertime,
or painting the same flower over and over with sloppy watercolor
and laying the soaking pages out to dry in the grass.

I am not as far away from who I was then
as you might like to think.
I know it was easier to love me before this.
You were once easier to love, too. But here we are now.
I am here to honor the past and run headlong into the future,
and I want you to be there with me.

That leaves us with only the matter of the present,
fingers knit in prayer, or worry, or gratitude.
I want you to know that I will keep on going,
living for everything we have left,
whether you come with me or not.

I want to write a poem for the women in my family

who never let me beat them at Scrabble,
who never went to college but stayed up late
to read the dictionary cover to cover.
Once, when I was ten, my grandmother beat me by 72 points.
The women in my family are ruthless.
They count syllables like kills
and never let me learn to play dumb.

I want to write a poem for the women in my family
who let their husbands call them crazy
for staying awake at night waiting for their sons to come home.
The same husbands who gave their daughters a curfew
and taught them how to break a chokehold in the backyard.
I want to write a poem for the women in my family who swear
they'll let their husbands die
if they won't stop eating red meat like the doctors said to,
but sneak crushed up vitamins into the beer bottles
when the men aren't looking.

I want to write a poem for the women in my family who used to tell me
we were related to the unsinkable Molly Brown,
but still insisted I take swimming lessons.
Who said, *sure you'll float, but what good is that if you're dead*?
I want to write a poem for the women in my family who did not survive
but still watch over me through candle flames and tarot cards.
I want to write a poem for the women in my family who hope and pray
that my poems are just stories,
but know that they are not.

I want to write a poem for my mother,
who still keeps my baby girl teeth in a box in her closet
because she can't throw her own child's bones in the garbage.
I want to write a poem for my mother who,
when I apologized for starving the good body she gave me,
cried with me.
I want to write a poem for my mother, who said,
baby, don't you ever say you're sorry.
Said *baby, this eating disorder runs through the women in our family*
like a goddamn forest fire
but baby you and I,
we are going to survive.
I want to write a poem for my mother, who said,
baby it's not your fault you were sick.
Baby, the whole world is sick.
I want to write a poem for my mother who said,
baby, of course I still love you.
Said *baby, me too.*

I love myself like this

Ruby light reflecting off my skin,
sunflower hazel eyes turned
curious searchlights, unworried
dime-sized mirrors.
Rib rolls spilling out
from under a crop top.
Soft-center girl,
hourglass of smooth sand
grains slipping past each other
as the glass rolls across the wood floor.

I have never been a moment older than this body,
but I have always felt like it.
I am always trying to tell you what I mean,
but now,
I am alive and safe
in this body
and I am learning to show you.

PART 4

A poet writes in solitude
after Micah Bournes

I'm afraid of living off of memory alone.
I used to write poems about people I loved and new places I went to
but now all I do is try to raise the dead,
to dredge up something within me that is worth resurrecting.
All I have are the things I remember
and I only have the things I remember
the way I remember them.

I'm afraid I'm just watching kaleidoscope dancers
through tinted sunglasses.
I'm afraid I'm cherry picking through my own past life
and falling in love with the story.
I'm afraid I'm becoming my own audience,
a belly full of mirrors.
I'm afraid this book is turning into a funhouse graveyard.
I'm afraid that everyone else will see me more than I can see myself.
I'm afraid of who I become when I am left alone
to tell the stories without corrections.
I'm afraid of forsaking my altar to reality
for some other new feeling.

I'm afraid of deciding what the truth is.
I'm afraid I am giving up on everything except the ghosts.
I'm not afraid of the people who will tell me I'm lying.
I'm afraid that somewhere, some part of me is.

Show me your wings

My father rode his motorcycle home
on the only day we had butterflies this year.
He came home covered in yellow gold slaughter.
He told me LA had never been so beautiful
and full of wings.

When I was young,
my grandparents had a cabin
in the mountains,
up a windy road that always made me sick.
My grandfather set off moth bombs
in the empty house every year,
but some always survived.
Brown-gray and wispy and gnawing
our clothes in the closets,
though my mother promised they didn't bite.

I wonder if I know what it means
to be cut from the ugly side of the cloth,
or if it matters to be called beautiful
if they will kill you anyway.

Aftertaste

My father and I are sitting in our rental car
in the church parking lot at my cousin's Mormon wedding,
pouring whiskey from a brown bag into paper cups
when he sits back and says,
Well, there goes my father of the year award again.

And it's not that we even want to be drunk,
we just both hate being told what not to do.
We hate spending more time than we need to
in a church that would spit us both out
if it knew where our scars came from.

To paint a picture of my father would be
to attempt a self-portrait painted
with hard lines and no shadows.
To shape a statue of my own soul,
but with all of the therapy scraped off
and all of the tears drained back into the skull

I tell him there is no award,
I think, *there is only surviving*, and here we are.
Here I am.
We don't talk about the wedding
because we don't want to talk about me,
about how maybe I don't love men enough
to ever wear a white dress,
or how he can't give someone away
who has always been running.

We go back inside without finishing our drinks.
We don't talk about it,
but we both revel in the rebel
of a half-empty sin in the cupholder,
in having a reason to return.

another god

Maybe there is another universe
where a god exists for me.
A god who will say,
Child, let us split this heartbreak
right down the middle
like an unripe peach
and only carry what we need to.
Who will say, *Child,*
I beat the rhythm of your heart
into your chest
with my own hands.
I shaped you not like me,
but like you.
Who will say,
I gave you everything
I thought you'd need.
Let me take away
some of what you didn't.

Albuquerque: For MindWell
After Sarah McMahon

On my last pre-Covid trip
I remember how to fall in love again in Albuquerque.

Sleepy eyes and stomach full of Christmas in February,
I walk across the city to an abandoned pharmacy
following a neon pink sign glowing *DRUGS*.

The empty pharmacy is really an open mic full of strangers,
and the strangers are really all poets, ready to open themselves
wide enough to love me back.

I don't know Zach, but it's his birthday and he's a Pisces
so his eyes well up a little
when we sing to him and slice the cake.

We spend the evening making space for each other.
I am asked to be the sacrificial poet for the slam
and I have never been so safe.

I know no other version of this city,
but I wish all sacrifices felt like a Friday night in Albuquerque
where strangers swap secrets
in a once-empty room.

Moment of grace

Ode to my cousin who remembered to wish me happy birthday
after a 12-hour shift in the Covid wing at her hospital.

Ode to the mask and goggle lines, pressed into her cheeks
and keeping her alive.

Ode to the echo of pots and pans banging from balconies
at each hospital shift change.

Her job is a study in forgiveness.
How many times can you drive past a crowded shopping mall
and keep trying to save everyone?

How many times can you witness the rest of us on our worst days,
help us Facetime our loved ones for their last moments
and then go on with the healing?

Ode to a depth of grace
we will never know how to deserve.

Sorry I missed your Zoom party

No, I have not fallen off the face of the Earth
even though this year keeps birthing days that make me want to.
But thank you for calling and checking
and noticing the radio silence.

A void wouldn't text me first so
there must be something more here
than my serotonin levels want me to believe.

The sun must wonder if he has any real friends,
since everyone he knows spins so close to him
but never stops to chat.
The moon must wonder if we'd would still love her
if she stopped pulling the ocean back
from swallowing us every morning.

I don't think I understand the relationship
between love and gravity,
but I know I am still here because of all of you.
My wings are damp, but unpinned.
I am not held down.
I am not held in place.
But still, I am held.

For Portland in summer

You are the second city I've ever loved enough
to not let a heartbreak eclipse your every bright spot.
Marionberry ice cream and lavender syrup
wash down any bitter aftertaste you leave.
Warm rain all May, rose city all summer,
you are the pinkest place I know.

The tall pink-mirrored tower
shines your reflection back at both of us.
Rosé at Joe's wine bar downtown,
strawberry sprinkle Homer donuts,
rose gardens and petal-pink snow cones.
Cotton candy pride parade,
girls with pink lips and nose rings,
blush of a new love and then
swollen eyes for a lost one.

You are pretty in October orange
and elegant January grey,
but I love you most in June
when we are both a little new.

In Portland, fat rain drops
rinse blood off the streets before it stains.
You are always hiding something behind your back,
some dirty secret lodged in your pink throat.
I do not know the whole of you
but you know all of me.

I look at you and you shine back
like rose-colored glasses,
lenses popped out and replaced
with two-way mirrors.

November 3

In sleep,
America dreams herself beautiful.
Skin smooth as fresh concrete
with no cracks for dandelions
to heave themselves up through.

No shadow in the evening of her cheekbones.
No still-warm skeletons
spilling out of her rib cage.
No voices crushed
in the hollow of her throat.

When she wakes
she looks out the red-blue
stained glass window
which shines her reflection back
in bruised purple.

They love me,
she screams at the peeling paint.
They really love me.

Directions for reemerging

What does it mean to bloom?
To open your eyes
wider than you could yesterday?

To peel off the armor
and reach toward the sky
with your softest parts first?

Nature only lets the average rosebud live loud
for two weeks before withering,
falling away to make room
for someone new.

But here you are,
trying to splay yourself open
for hundreds of seasons at once,
like your mothers never taught you cycle
or sleep.

Let us teach ourselves a new love
that is more forest than branches,
more trust than slice open
to count the rings.
Let ours
be a chorus of hearts knit together
with daisy chains and sunlight.

But really,
before we start the braid
what does it mean to bloom here?
In the ashes of our old lives?
Let me be more clear.

You must pull yourself out by the roots.
Leave the rotten behind,
but open your jaw wide enough
to swallow the dirt that made you.

There is no grow,
no progress,
no unpeel or bloom without
a rearview mirror,
a burden of bloodline or consequence.
You inherited the gold and the gun.
You can be nothing without whatever ugly
you came from,
so hold grateful and angry between your teeth.
But now,

now is the time for dancing,
for disentangling the roots that choked
someone else,
for shaking the fruit from your own body
to feed on.
Now, you can suck the poison
back out from the water.

You cannot abandon yourself
or the ghosts who watched you grow up,
but whatever runs through your veins
doesn't have to flow from your mouth.
If we have always moved by river
let us teach ourselves to love like reservoir,

but only for a moment.
There is no such thing as bloom without
untangle and lose.
Good love has never been still or silent.

When the revolution comes,
a tidal wave foaming at the mouth
and full of life,
spill into it.
You will not be ready,
but reach
or bloom
or run to it,
old and new roots
dragging behind your bare feet.

Pull as many hands as you can
along with you.
Let your new ears unfold like petals
while you follow the music.

This is the only way up.

I get the vaccine and drive to Pismo Beach

There are entire lives that begin and end
in the tidepools at Pismo Beach.

We climb sharp rocks just to bend over finger-deep water
and peer in, like untrained gods studying someone else's work.

What are we going to do with all this death?

At dusk, the sun paints a rainbow sherbet sky
above the soft blue water

like a heterochromatic butterfly with a horizon for a spine.
or a half-dipped ice cream cone.

What are we going to do with all this death?

We all sit far apart, look up, and breathe in
like the world we used to know is still out there.

Like back home, LA didn't spend last Christmas
with suspended air quality control laws

to give crematories a chance
to burn through the backlog of bodies.

What are we going to do with all this death?

I get the vaccine and have another identity crisis on the drive home from Pismo Beach

What are we going to do with all this new?

I came to this beach two years ago in a different body,
a different life with a different future.

A drive up the 101 is a drive past all the people I used to be,
like a linear catalog of my early twenties.

We pass restaurants and bars and beaches
where I remember leaving pieces of myself behind

like shedding old skin,
but not always becoming better.

I go back to the best coffeeshop in Carpinteria
and reintroduce my weight to the creaky wood deck outside.

I walk past what used to be my favorite bar in Ventura,
before they filled it with flowers and fixed the broken glass.

When a tadpole becomes a frog, it is not more beautiful.
I replace one ghost with another.

Time has always passed,
and I have always changed.

But more than a year spent inside the four walls of myself
feels like something more than time.

I have closed so many books.
Forgotten old limbs and grown new ones.

I know I won't fit in all the places where
I used to feel at home anymore.

What are we going to do with all this new?

I think I am becoming less like all the things I used to point to
and more like myself.

I don't know what that will mean
when it comes time to show everyone else.

Addendum to Directions for reemerging

Before I can bloom,
I have to pull myself out by the roots,
fall muddy and unsafe out of
the deepest parts of my lineage,
pack myself into a single petal to be caught up in the wind
and taken somewhere new.

Before I can bloom,
I have to face myself.
How can I learn to love the person I am
before I am the person I want to be
and while I am still the person built by
all the things I want to leave behind?

my love, the world is ending

I promise I did my best to stop it.
I recycled.
I bought you a reusable water bottle,
planted and raised herbs and succulents
everywhere I could,
wore a thrift store jacket on our first date.
If anyone could compost enough
wilted spinach leaves
to nurse the planet back to health
I would have done it, just for you.

My love,
I went to the protests.
I voted for the ones
who seemed less evil
and still
the world is ending.

I don't know what will come first.
Maybe the ocean,
warm and swelling
like our bodies used to be together,
or the trees,
burning and ascending to a new life,
leaving us gasping and heaving.

Or maybe
the carcinogens,
chemicals, and dyes
we've been feeding
each other for years
will turn everyone to zombies
before the ocean swallows us
for our sins.

If you go first,
I think I will still feel lucky
when you walk toward me,
stiff and hungry.
I will still kiss the tips of your ears
whisper I love you
while you go for my brain,
jaw wide.

And I think I will feel special.
My love,
the world is ending
and you still want to know
what I'm thinking.

What will I do when I run out of things to say?

Will I still be a writer when the writing is finished?
Will anyone sit next to me on the porch,
coffee cups in hand,
and listen to me try to make something new
out of all the things
I've already explained before?

When we run out of poems,
when everything there is to say
has be written and then rewritten,
will we just tell each other the same stories over and over
until we have memorized them all?
And say, *yes, I have heard this before,*
yes, I remember,
but tell me again.
It sounds better when you read it.

This is why I don't write poems about you

If we only get one planet,
if all the stardust we used to be
has found each other
to take shape for just a moment,
to spin in the same circles
for a handful of cycles
all of this will be enough.

I have always believed in love
but I have never believed in soulmates.
I don't want to believe I was made
for anything or anyone
and you have never asked me to.

In this love,
we are always taking turns
sliding from one seat to the next
to teach the other
this is how to love me,
and then, to listen.

Our love is more salt than anchor,
more tide pool than tempest,
all sparkle and soft blue ripple.
This is the way I want to see the world,
holding your familiar hands
in all the unfamiliar oceans.

If the purpose of poetry
is to help other people
understand an experience they cannot have,
then the world should wish
I never have to write a poem about you.
If poetry is an exercise in restraint,
then I will never write a poem about the way I love you,
I'll just live in it.

I wish this for everyone,
but the best I can do
is hold this love close
to both our open hearts
like salve,
rebraiding all the frayed ends
that lead back to all the life
we are always blooming into.

Ode to Fat Bottomed Girls

It is Saturday night and Freddie Mercury and I
are sprawled separate on my couch swiping through tinder.
We swap stories about bad dates and good kissers.
A boy messages me about my red hair and we laugh
while a girl messages him about his smile—
crescent enough to fill the whole frame.
He says he really did love her,
and I believe him.
I tell him that I cannot sing
but that I too have called the sun a lover.
We have both believed in forever more than once.

He gave himself a grounding name.
Virgo boy who chose the hot side of his own planet.
There is logic in this.
I could call myself Christina Venus,
admit at every introduction that my heart rules my body,
try to live up to a name that takes after a place I don't know
and a heat I can't handle,
and this is not the same thing.

I am pretending not to see any of the girls
with bios that say, "lesbians only."
We talk about how it feels to tell a lover
who you are, only to be corrected,
to know they will cut you in half and still swallow you whole.
How the audience only accepts your wholeness
when you are making art about being broken.

I ask him if he thinks bisexuality is really just a phase,
and he says *honey of course,*
what else could our bodies possibly be?
Do not tell me you don't sing and scream and mumble and hide
the way the moon does.
What is a body if not the love it wants?
What is the love you want if not the moon
spinning around everything she knows
believing that circles mean forever when we know
even the sun will burn out?

Freddie says *they will tell you who you are*
and you will show them.
It is up to you to decide who to believe.

GIRL TEETH

ACKNOWLEDGEMENTS

Special thanks to my family for raising me, to my friends for holding me, and to my partner, Sidney, who is the kindest person I know.

Thank you to the following publications, who published earlier versions of the following poems:

"Sex Robot Elegy," published as "Why I Care About Sex Robots" in *Fight Evil with Poetry Volume I* and *The American Papers*.

"I wish my body were a poem," published in Brave Voices Magazine.

"A Study of Fear as a Houseplant" published in The Bridge Volume II.

"Directions for Reemerging" published as "There is No Such Thing as Bloom" by Level Ground Co. Adapted to film by meredith adelaide.

"Ode to Fat Bottomed Girls" published in *SKEW Magazine*.

Thank you to all of my newsletter subscribers, who help sustain my writing. Special thanks to annual subscribers:

Chelsee Bergen
Nick Catt
Sidney Karanja
Ryan Stevens
Lindsay Miklovich
Nila Brown
Irene Betsch
Kelly Demory
Karen Han
Livia Kim
Benin Lemus
Alyssa Matuchniak

www.ingramcontent.com/pod-product-compliance
Lightning Source LLC
Chambersburg PA
CBHW021012090426
42738CB00007B/765